ARISTOTLE

THE FATHER OF LOGIC

THE GREATEST GREEK PHILOSOPHERS

ARISTOTLE

THE FATHER OF LOGIC

KELLY ROSCOE & MICK ISLE

ROSEN PUBLISHING
NEW YORK

Published in 2016 by The Rosen Publishing Group, Inc.
29 East 21st Street, New York, NY 10010

First Edition

Library of Congress Cataloging-in-Publication Data

Roscoe, Kelly, author.
Aristotle : the father of logic/Kelly Roscoe and Mick Isle.—First edition.
pages cm.—(The greatest Greek philosophers)
Includes bibliographical references and index.
ISBN 978-1-4994-6126-8 (library bound)
1. Aristotle—Juvenile literature. 2. Philosophers—Greece—Biography—Juvenile literature. 3. Scientists—Greece—Biography—Juvenile literature. 4. Philosophy, Ancient—Juvenile literature. I. Isle, Mick, author. II. Title.
B481.R625 2016
185—dc23
[B]

2014043157

Manufactured in the United States of America

Contents

INTROD

Though Aristotle lived more than two thousand years ago in the fourth century BCE, his ideas on topics ranging from philosophy and reasoning to science and politics were highly influential to Western civilization. Up until the Renaissance, he was considered the greatest thinker in human history, and he remains a significant philosopher today, despite the fact that some of his theories turned out to be inaccurate.

Aristotle was able to thrive intellectually because he migrated to Athens at the age of seventeen, in 367 BCE. At that time, Athens had already been a destination for artists, craftsmen, and scholars for centuries. By 800 BCE, the city was the leader in a new commercial, military, and cultural revival across Greece. Athens grew so powerful that it became a city-state, with its own government, army, laws, and traditions. During this time, similar city-states emerged in various parts of Greece. They founded their own colonies—some as far away as Spain, Egypt, and the Ukraine—and became quite wealthy. They sometimes cooperated through trade, though they also often fought wars against each other. Aside from Athens, the other most powerful city was Sparta, which became Athens's major rival.

Aristotle and other immigrants came to take advantage of Athens's economic and educational opportunities as well as the many freedoms enjoyed by its citizens. Other Greek cities, such as Sparta,

UCTION

This Roman bust of Aristotle from the second century BCE is a copy of a Greek bust from c. 325 BCE, only a few years after his death.

CHAPTER ONE

A Boy from Stagira

Although many of Aristotle's ideas have survived the thousands of years since he lived, historians know little about his life, especially his childhood. Aristotle was born in 384 BCE in Stagira, a small town in northern Greece, close to the kingdom of Macedonia and around 175 miles (281 kilometers) from Athens. His father, Nicomachus, was a well-respected doctor who came from a long line of physicians. His mother, Phaestis, was from a wealthy family that lived on the island of Euboea, in southern Greece. Aristotle also had a brother, Arimnestus, and a sister, Arimneste, both of whom were thought to be older than he was.

EARLY EDUCATION

Aristotle probably began school when he was around six. Most likely, he went to a neighborhood school where he learned how to read, write, and do arithmetic. Instead of a blackboard or paper, students practiced writing by scratching letters onto a wax-covered wooden block with a sharpened stick. To figure out math calculations, students counted with pebbles or a wooden tool called an abacus.

In ancient times, abaci such as this one from China were used all over the world for counting and arithmetic.

At school, boys learned how to play flutes and small harps called lyres, which were both very popular instruments in ancient Greece. Boys also studied literature and poetry. The most famous of all Greek poems were two enormous tales by Homer: *The Iliad* and *The Odyssey*. Students had to memorize long passages—sometimes hundreds of lines—and recite them in class. During their teenage years, they practiced the art of rhetoric, or public speaking. The ability

RHETORIC

Rhetoric comes from the Greek for "orator," or public speaker. In modern times, the concept of rhetoric has expanded to include both oral and written communication. Long after he first practiced public speaking as a schoolboy, Aristotle wrote *Rhetoric*, an influential treatise on the topic. The purpose of rhetoric is for the speaker to persuade the audience. Aristotle outlined three different means of persuasion: a speaker can make credible arguments (ethos), appeal to the audience's emotions (pathos), or use logic and reasoning (logos).

Aristotle focused on the importance of choosing the right words and organizing the argument; he did not give much advice in *Rhetoric* on the actual delivery of the speech.

to argue and debate using sophisticated vocabulary and a dramatic speaking style was a valued trait in ancient Greek society. Those who mastered the art of rhetoric were widely respected and admired.

Outside school, Aristotle was probably tutored at home by his father. It was common practice in ancient Greece for doctors to teach their sons about science and medicine. As a young boy, Aristotle probably learned a fair bit about human anatomy and diseases by observing Nicomachus at work. He likely accompanied his father when he went searching for medicinal plants and herbs that were used as remedies for common ailments such as stomachaches and fevers. These early experiences might help account for Aristotle's later interest in natural sciences—biology, botany, and zoology. In ancient Greece, the profession of physician was passed down directly from father to son. It was thus probable that Nicomachus was training Aristotle to be a doctor.

When Aristotle was still very young, King Amyntas II of Macedonia hired Nicomachus to be his personal physician. The men in Aristotle's family had a long tradition of serving as physicians to Macedonian kings. At the Macedonian royal court, Aristotle made friends with the king's youngest son, Philip, who was roughly the same age.

When Aristotle was ten years old, his father died, and his mother died shortly after. Suddenly an orphan, young Aristotle was taken in and raised by a close friend of his father's, Proxenus, who lived in the city of Atarneus. Leaving behind his medical apprenticeship, the teenage Aristotle spent much of his time studying poetry and rhetoric.

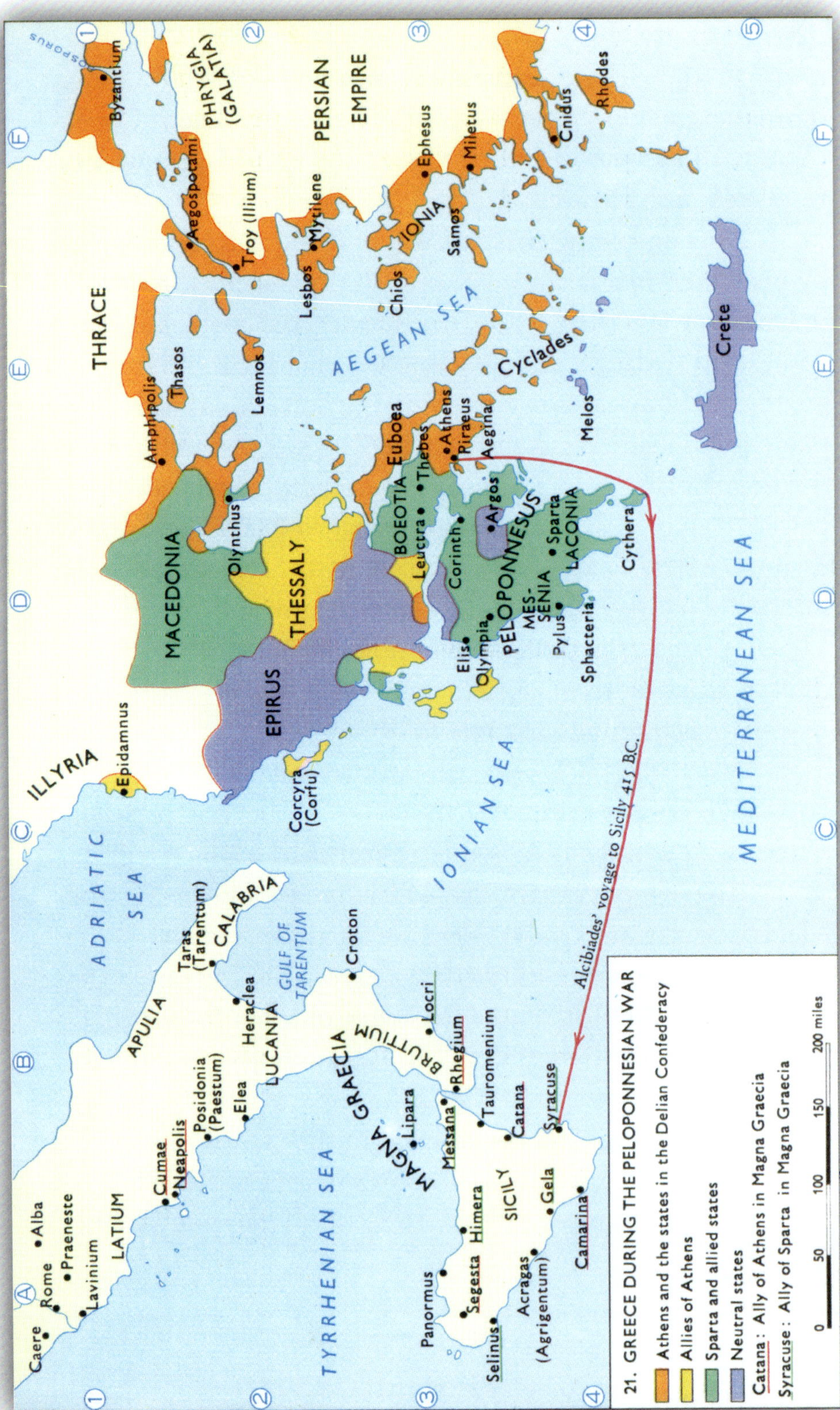

21. GREECE DURING THE PELOPONNESIAN WAR
Athens and the states in the Delian Confederacy
Allies of Athens
Sparta and allied states
Neutral states
Catana : Ally of Athens in Magna Graecia
Syracuse : Ally of Sparta in Magna Graecia
0 50 100 150 200 miles
Alcibiades' voyage to Sicily 415 B.C.
THRACE
PHRYGIA (GALATIA)
PERSIAN EMPIRE
MACEDONIA
THESSALY
EPIRUS
ILLYRIA
BOEOTIA
PELOPONNESUS
LACONIA
MES-SENIA
IONIA
AEGEAN SEA
IONIAN SEA
MEDITERRANEAN SEA
ADRIATIC SEA
TYRRHENIAN SEA
GULF OF TARENTUM
MAGNA GRAECIA
SICILY
LATIUM
APULIA
CALABRIA
LUCANIA
BRUTTIUM
Byzantium
Aegospotami
Troy (Ilium)
Lesbos
Mytilene
Chios
Samos
Ephesus
Miletus
Cnidus
Rhodes
Cyclades
Melos
Crete
Thasos
Lemnos
Amphipolis
Olynthus
Euboea
Thebes
Athens
Piraeus
Aegina
Leuctra
Corinth
Argos
Sparta
Cythera
Olympia
Elis
Pylus
Sphacteria
Epidamnus
Corcyra (Corfu)
Taras (Tarentum)
Heraclea
Croton
Locri
Rhegium
Messana
Tauromenium
Catana
Syracuse
Lipara
Elea
Posidonia (Paestum)
Cumae
Neapolis
Caere
Rome
Alba
Praeneste
Lavinium
Panormus
Segesta
Himera
Selinus
Acragas (Agrigentum)
Gela
Camarina

Shortly after Aristotle's parents' deaths, King Amyntas died, too. As a result of the king's death, Macedonia experienced a period of upheaval with armed political rebellions that lasted several years. Proxenus must have felt that amid this unstable environment, Aristotle would have a difficult time securing his future. Therefore, when he was seventeen, Aristotle was sent to continue his studies in the great city of Athens.

ATHENIAN SOCIETY

The site upon which the city of Athens was built had been inhabited since prehistoric times. Surrounded by protective mountains, its acropolis—the Greek word for "high place"—provided sweeping views of the surrounding plains and sea. The Mycenaeans had decided to build a fortified settlement on the rocky acropolis for strategic purposes. Over time, this initial settlement grew into a city called Athinai. Its name honored the city's protectress: Athena, the Greek goddess of wisdom.

Crowning the acropolis was the Parthenon, an impressive temple devoted to Athena. It was the city's most important religious monument. Inside the temple was a 40-foot (12-meter) statue of Athena, made entirely of gold and ivory. At the bottom of the acropolis was the Theater of Dionysus, built in honor of the Greek god of wine

This map shows the various states of Greece in the fifth century BCE. Aristotle's hometown, Stagira, was near Macedonia and is part of present-day Greece.

Among the ancient structures that still survive on the acropolis of Athens are the Parthenon and the Erechtheum, both temples dedicated to Athena, and the odeon of Herodes Atticus, an amphitheater.

and celebration. Here, audiences watched plays or musical performances while sitting in an amphitheater (a half circle of stone benches built into the hillside). At the time, drama festivals, sponsored by city taxes, were very popular. Wealthy Athenians also helped pay performers' fees and considered it an honor to donate money to the arts.

Between the sixth and fifth centuries BCE, Athens became a renowned center of literature and the arts. Many of ancient Greece's greatest playwrights and poets were living in Athens. Writers such as Aeschylus, Aristophanes, Euripides, Simonides, and Sophocles (author of the play

The playwright Euripides (c. 484 BCE–406 BCE) wrote many tragedies, including Alcestis, Medea, Children of Heracles, *and* Hippolyta.

Oedipus the King) produced some of the most powerful works in Western literature.

Although Athens in the fifth century BCE had a population of roughly 320,000 people, only around 50,000 were considered Athenian citizens with full rights, such as the right to vote and participate in public life. Almost a third of Athenian society was made up of slaves. Men and women were born into slavery or became slaves after being captured in wars between Athens and other city-states or kingdoms.

Although slaves had to do the most difficult work, they were generally treated much better and enjoyed more freedoms in Athens than in other Greek cities. Some received wages with which they could eventually buy their freedom. Others, who worked in the homes of the wealthy, were treated like members of the family. In fact, foreigners criticized Athens because they said it was difficult to tell the difference between slaves and free citizens. Outside Athens, it was often believed that slaves were inferior beings who didn't deserve to be treated like humans.

Women also did not have rights as citizens. They could not vote, walk in the streets, or even take part in theatrical productions (female roles were played by males). Because they were expected to grow up and become wives and mothers, girls didn't go to school. Instead, they stayed at home where their mothers taught them how to weave fabrics, sew clothing, and cook. These tasks were necessary since most girls would be married and start to raise families by the age of fifteen or sixteen.

Metics, the name given to men from other cities who immigrated to Athens, were also denied the political rights of Athenian citizens. Although they were free, they could not participate in political assemblies, nor could they vote. Aristotle, too, was considered a *metic* because he was foreign-born (from Stagira). Even though he did not have as many rights as Athenian citizens, Athens provided Aristotle with the opportunity to learn from the most admired thinkers of the time.

Soon, Aristotle joined a great tradition of ancient Greek philosophers who transformed Western thinking by asking fundamental questions and then seeking answers based on logical reasoning and scientific observation. He studied at the Academy, a school that had quickly built a reputation as a distinguished center of learning due to the reputation of its founder, director, and principal teacher—the great philosopher Plato.

CHAPTER TWO

IN THE SHADOW OF SOCRATES AND PLATO

Just as Aristotle was to become Plato's most accomplished pupil, Plato himself had studied under Socrates, one of the first and greatest of the ancient Greek philosophers. Socrates' most important contribution to Western thought was his method of inquiry, or asking questions. Philosophers in this era considered four major questions as they attempted to understand the world around them:

- Where do things (living and non-living) come from?
- What are they made of?
- How does one explain so many different things in nature?
- How can one describe all of these things?

The rational methods they used to answer these questions laid the foundations for modern philosophy and science.

THE SOCRATIC METHOD

An Athenian citizen, Socrates was born in 469 BCE. His father was a stonemason, and his mother was a midwife. As an adult, Socrates compared his role as a philosopher to that of a midwife. However, in his analogy, instead of helping give birth to a baby, he delivered the truth.

Socrates grew up while Athens was at the height of its power and influence as a cultural and intellectual center. As a young man, he spent much time in the streets of Athens, where the great thinkers and artists of the day debated their advanced ideas in public. Even once he was an adult and married, Socrates continued to spend time in Athens's lively marketplaces or at banquets in private homes. Here, intellectual debates were carried on for hours at a time. His wife was apparently angered by his frequent absences from home. However, Socrates's socializing gave him the opportunity to indulge in his favorite intellectual activity: questioning people about what they knew—and didn't.

A true "lover of wisdom," Socrates became obsessed with discovering truths about the world. Even though he was considered by many to be the wisest man in Athens, Socrates believed he was quite ignorant

This fresco of Socrates dates back to the first century BCE *and hangs in the Ephesus Archaeological Museum in Selçuk, Turkey.*

Works such as *The Clouds* provide the best evidence of Socrates's philosophy, since he did not write down any of his ideas during his lifetime. Socrates' students Plato and Xenophon also portrayed their teacher in various works. Though their portrayals of Socrates may be idealized, they are the most accurate accounts that have survived from antiquity. In his Socratic dialogues, Plato demonstrated the Socratic method of inquiry: continual questioning of a person until, through inevitable contradictions, the person's ideas were proved wrong. This form of questioning was called *elenchus* by both Socrates and Plato.

SOCRATES'S TRIAL AND DEATH

In 399 BCE, the Athenian court of justice accused Socrates of corrupting the city's youth. Socrates, who was seventy at the time, argued that his teaching young Athenians to question life had, in fact, been very positive. In his famous work *Apology*, Plato recorded the self-defense that Socrates gave to the jury at his trial:

French artist Jacques-Louis David's 1787 painting The Death of Socrates *shows Socrates bravely accepting the cup of hemlock that would kill him.*

> To put it bluntly I've been assigned to this city as if to a large horse which is inclined to be lazy and is in need of some great stinging fly and all day long I'll never cease to settle here, there, everywhere, rousing and reproving every one of you.

Angered by the candor of this statement, the jury found Socrates guilty. In keeping with Athenian tradition, the accuser and the accused were asked to propose a penalty. The accuser proposed death, while Socrates declared that he should receive the city's highest honors. These were usually only reserved for Olympic athletes. Enraged by what they viewed as excessive pride, the jury gave him the extreme punishment the accuser had requested.

Socrates's last days were spent in jail, where he was visited by many friends and students. He refused to take part in friends' plans to help him escape from prison and faced his death without fear. As friends wept openly, Socrates drank the cup of poisonous hemlock that killed him.

SOCRATES'S SUCCESSOR

One of Socrates's most devoted young students was Plato. Plato's real name was Aristocles. He was born in 427 BCE to a wealthy Athenian family. The nickname Plato was acquired during his adolescence when he practiced the popular sport of wrestling. From the Greek word for "broad," *Plato* likely referred to young Aristocles' muscular physique.

At the age of twenty, Plato began studying with Socrates. Like other teachers, Socrates held classes outdoors in the streets and marketplaces of Athens, where students would gather around and listen to him. Socrates was a great influence on young Plato. When Socrates was sentenced to death, Plato attended his trial. Many of his earliest writings record his memories of his teacher, including his trial and death.

Both of these events affected Plato deeply. He felt that Socrates had been the victim of a great injustice. He was so angered by the role of Athens's democratic government in Socrates's death that he left the city after the philosopher's execution. Much of Plato's later writings on politics and ethics reflected his search for an ideal society where such injustices wouldn't occur. In fact, in his most renowned work, *The Republic* (written in his later years, circa 360 BCE), Plato proposes a form of government ruled by philosophers. His most famous written works were composed in the form of dialogues between two or more speakers with different points of view. They were based on the long question-and-answer sessions that Socrates had used as his method of inquiry. Often, the main character in these written debates was Socrates himself. As such, many of Socrates's ideas were faithfully recorded.

After Socrates's death, Plato spent the next twelve years traveling throughout Greece, Egypt, Italy, and Sicily. Aside from many adventures—according to rumors, he was captured by pirates and sold as a slave—he learned a great deal. When he finally returned to Athens, he decided to continue Socrates's legacy as a teacher. However, instead of lecturing in the streets, he decided to buy a plot of land and open up a permanent

At the Academy, Plato taught his students outside in the olive grove.

school. This would become the first university in the Western world.

The land Plato purchased, an olive grove, had once belonged to an Athenian named Academos. In his honor, Plato called his school the Academy (which, in turn, became the origin of the English word "academics"). Even though there were buildings where students could sleep and eat, classes were held outdoors beneath the trees.

Plato's aim was to teach numerous subjects ranging from politics and philosophy to mathematics and medicine. Attracted by Plato's fame and the school's mission, students from all over Greece came to study at the Academy. No examinations or diplomas were given; students studied simply because they wanted to gain knowledge.

As a philosopher, Plato wrote on subjects as varied as science, mathematics, justice, government, love, and the notion of the human soul. He was also concerned with the pursuit of virtue in politics and art and among human beings. In *The Republic*, he described his ideal city-state, in which all citizens have a specific job (tailor, farmer, banker, wife, etc.) allowing them to contribute to the wealth, success, and harmony of society. He also examined different types of government, such as monarchy and democracy, in an attempt to determine which one was the most virtuous. Ultimately, he proposed

a state ruled by wise and well-educated "philosopher-kings." As described in *The Republic*, these were "men . . . perfected by years and education." Having viewed the way the Athenian assembly had turned on his mentor, Socrates, he was very critical of democracy.

IDEALS VS. REALITY

One of Plato's most important contributions to philosophy was the way he viewed reality. Plato believed that all things in the world were present in two forms. Ideal, or subjective, forms can be understood but cannot be detected by human senses. (For instance, one can understand the idea of air, although air cannot be seen, heard, or touched.) In contrast, perceptual, or objective,

The construction of a building is an example of Plato's two forms. The architect's ideal vision in the blueprints inevitably differs from the perceptual final product. This is Meredith Hall at Drake University in Iowa.

forms (for example, water) can be perceived by the human senses. Plato demonstrated this notion using the example of a carpenter about to make a chair. Because of his knowledge, in his mind, the carpenter has an image of an ideal chair he plans to make. But this imagined chair is never the same as the real, physical chair he ends up constructing. Furthermore, if the carpenter makes fifty chairs, none will be the same due to the differences in wood, the tools used, and the care taken by the carpenter. Chairs, like all objects, therefore exist in two forms: the perfect or ideal chair and the real chairs that carpenters actually make that can be sat upon.

Plato viewed the entire physical world in this manner. For instance, the idea of a dog conjured up in someone's head is different from the various types of dogs that people own as pets. This distinction led Plato to believe that the world was created by a perfect craftsman known as God. Inspired by perfect forms, this creator made everything in

THE ROLE OF ART IN SOCIETY

Both Aristotle and Plato viewed art as a mimesis (the origin of the English words "mime" and "mimic"), or imitation, of nature. However, Plato felt this imitation was negative. For example, a painting of a bed could never hope to provide a substitute for an actual bed. As such, art was seen as inferior, merely a cheap imitation that was neither useful nor informative. Unsurprisingly, in Plato's *Republic*, in which he outlined his ideal society, artists possessed no useful function. Plato even suggested they be banished. He believed that artists were dangerous to society because they relied on lies and illusions and provoked emotions that interfered with people's rational thoughts.

In contrast, Aristotle viewed mimesis as being positive. In one of his most renowned works, Poetics (circa 350 bce), he wrote that art completes what nature cannot finish. By this he meant that, for example, a painting of a bed represented more than a simple object. Depending on the artist's imagination and skill, this representation could project new types and uses of beds. In this sense, art wasn't simply reproducing something that already existed but rather reinventing other potential realities. As such, the artist became a useful member of society whose work resulted in new inventions and ways of thinking. Aristotle also viewed people's emotional reactions to works of art as something positive. He claimed that a person's pleasure in art was equal to the pleasure felt in learning something new about the world.

This tile from the Santa Maria del Fiore Church in Florence, Italy, depicts Aristotle in deep philosophical discussion with Plato.

the world as copies or images of them. This vision of the world came to be known as Platonism.

LEARNING FROM A MASTER

By the time Aristotle began studying at the Academy, Plato was already considered one of Greece's most important philosophers. Aristotle was so eager to learn that his colleagues often called him Anagnostes, the Greek word for "the reader." Soon, Plato was referring to his bright student as "the intelligence of the school."

It wasn't long before Aristotle himself began teaching at the Academy. Aristotle greatly admired Plato, and the two had a close relationship. However, as time went by, Aristotle began to question some of Plato's views and develop a philosophy of his own.

CHAPTER THREE

The Student Becomes the Teacher

Over the almost twenty years that Aristotle spent at Plato's Academy, his rejection of many of Plato's ideas caused his teacher to say, "Aristotle spurns me as colts kick out the mother who bore them." Nevertheless, while the two men had conflicting ideas on many subjects, they maintained a great deal of admiration for each other.

TWO MODELS OF THE WORLD

The major conflict between Plato and Aristotle stemmed from Plato's belief in an ideal world that was a model of perfection and couldn't be detected by the senses. Aristotle believed in a physical world whose laws could be observed, measured, and investigated. He rejected the notion of a divine creator who made the universe out of unformed materials. Instead, Aristotle put forth the idea of a natural world with its own laws, order, and logic, which had been set into motion but not created by God. For instance, if one plants an acorn, one knows it will grow into an oak tree and not a birch

Plato and Aristotle are at the center of Raphael's famed work The School of Athens. *Plato, in purple and red robes, is pointing up, symbolizing his abstract work. Aristotle, in blue, has his hand facing the ground, symbolizing his work with nature.*

As a result of all these factors, Aristotle set off on a journey throughout Greece and Asia Minor (present-day Turkey). In Asia Minor, he visited the coastal city of Assos, where he was welcomed by King Hermias. Hermias, an old friend of Aristotle's and fellow student at the Academy, had started out very poor in life before rising to power. With the help of the neighboring king of Persia, King Artaxerxes, he succeeded in seizing the throne of Assos. Under his rule, Assos had developed into an important intellectual and cultural center, and Hermias encouraged his scholarly friend to settle in Assos and share his knowledge. Ultimately, Aristotle became director of a school of philosophy similar to the Academy. He then married Hermias's niece, Pythias, who was around eighteen at the time. Together, they had a daughter also named Pythias.

For the next few years, Aristotle and his new family lived in tranquility. However, during this time, Hermias began to become friendly with Philip of Macedonia.

King Artaxerxes, who had helped keep Hermias in power, was not pleased with this new alliance. In 344 BCE, the king invited Hermias to Persia. Instead of a friendly

Fishing is still an important source of income for residents of the island of Lesbos, where Aristotle moved after Hermias was killed.

visit, Hermias was taken prisoner, tortured, and crucified. Aristotle was devastated. Shortly after, he moved to Lesbos, a nearby island in the Aegean Sea, because he felt it was no longer safe for his family to remain in Assos.

On Lesbos, Aristotle became close friends with a young scholar named Theophrastus. Both men were fascinated by the study of the natural world. Theophrastus was interested in plant life. Meanwhile, Aristotle began to collect and study the sea creatures that lived in the warm Aegean waters. He soon extended his study of sea animals to all living creatures. On Lesbos, students, other teachers, and local fishermen helped him to collect new specimens. Travelers told him stories about animals they had encountered on their voyages. These tales, along with his own observations, helped him create detailed descriptions of many living creatures. At the time, this study of animals and their behavior was unheard of. Serious philosophers were supposed to be concerned with more "scientific" subjects, such as mathematics, ethics, and astronomy. Aristotle defended his passion by declaring that animals (aside from being just as fascinating) were easier to study than faraway stars.

A NATURAL SCIENTIST

Aristotle's study of living creatures led him to invent zoology, or the classification and study of animals. Aristotle was the first person to create a system of classifying animals according to their characteristics and habits. Over time, he gave names to and described more than five hundred types of animals.

Once he had observed and gathered information about creatures, Aristotle was able to divide them into types or species. The first major distinction he made was between "bloodless" animals—those without vertebrae or backbones—and "blooded" animals with backbones. These categories were then further subdivided as follows:

"Bloodless" Animals (Invertebrates)	"Blooded" Animals (Vertebrates)
Animals with soft exteriors (such as octopus and squid)	Human beings
Animals with armorlike hard exteriors that can be smashed (such as crabs and lobsters)	Birds
Animals with hard shell-like exteriors that must be hammered open (such as oysters and snails)	Four-footed animals that give birth to offspring (such as horses and dogs)
Insects	Four-footed animals that lay eggs (lizards)
	Fish that give birth to offspring (such as whales and dolphins)
	Fish that lay eggs (such as tuna and salmon)

The feeding apparatus of green sea urchins, the five hard plates seen in the middle of their undersides, shown here, is known as Aristotle's lantern, based on his observation of it.

Aristotle was aware that these broad categories were not perfect. For instance, he knew that while they lived in the sea and gave birth to their young in the water, whales and dolphins were technically mammals and not fish.

Frequently, Aristotle dissected the animals, cutting them open in order to study their internal organs, such as the heart, brain, and liver. The notes he took on animals included observations of their daily habits and behavior—how they hunted, mated, gave birth, and related to other creatures. Some of his descriptions, included in his published works *The History of Animals* (circa 350 BCE) and *On the Parts of Animals* (circa 350 BCE), were very lively. He wrote that elephants' trunks produced a noise like a hoarse trumpet and compared hyenas' cries to the noise of a man throwing up. He praised the octopus for its tidy housekeeping habits.

Aristotle also showed interest in human anatomy. Unfortunately, religious rules prohibited the dissection of humans and made studying the human body a complicated task. However, based on the animals he dissected, Aristotle made some conclusions about human beings. Over time, some of these turned out to be quite incorrect. He believed, for example, that the heart was the center of all intelligence, while the brain functioned as a type of air-conditioner to the heart, cooling the blood as it circulated throughout the body.

In exploring how an animal got along (or didn't) with other animals, adapted to the climate, and searched for food, water and shelter, Aristotle ended up making many observations about the animal's environment. In doing so, he was the first to link the study of living things to their natural habitats. This science later became known as ecology.

ARISTOTLE'S GREATEST STUDENT

After a year or two in Lesbos, Aristotle received an invitation from King Philip II of Macedonia. The king wanted the son of his father's former physician to come to his court at Pella and tutor his thirteen-year-old son, Alexander. Aristotle accepted the offer. Upon his arrival, he was pleased to discover that his new student was an exceptionally bright and curious young man.

Aristotle and Alexander quickly formed a close bond. Aside from natural history, Aristotle taught the young prince a great deal about politics, philosophy, and ethics—all of which were important subjects for a future king. He also taught him poetry, including the works of Homer. Alexander was particularly impressed by the action-filled *Iliad*. He memorized most of the sixteen thousand lines of this epic poem.

Aside from being intelligent, young Alexander was also very brave. Some time before Aristotle's arrival in Macedonia, he had formed a bond with a beautiful, wild horse that none of King Philip's stable hands could mount. He bet his father that he could ride the horse, and he won. King Philip was so proud of his son that he cried tears of joy. In his *Life of Alexander* (circa 100 CE), the Greek historian Plutarch (circa 45–125 CE) said the king cried, "O my son, look thee out a kingdom equal to and worthy of thyself,

Alexander (right) *listens to his teacher Aristotle in a palace in Pella, Greece, circa 342* BCE.

GREECE'S MOST FAMED POET

Considered one of the great poets of all times, Homer was thought to have lived in the eighth century bce. Almost nothing is known about his life aside from the fact that he was blind. In fact, some scholars wonder if he really existed or if he was only a legend. At the time Homer lived, poetry was spoken instead of written. Homer would have composed and memorized *The Iliad* and *The Odyssey* and then traveled throughout Greece reciting them to audiences. Over time, these poems became the two most important works in ancient Greek culture. They were recited and memorized by generations of Greeks.

Aside from their literary and historic value, these poems were also used as guides for moral behavior. The heroes' decisions and actions provided young Greeks with many lessons about honor, friendship, courage, and justice. Many Greek gods and goddesses, such as Apollo, Athena, and Aphrodite, appeared as characters in both poems, thus revealing the importance of religion in Greek life.

The Iliad tells the tale of the ten-year Trojan War fought between the Greeks and the Trojans, whose legendary city is situated in present-day Turkey. The war broke out after

Prince Paris of Troy kidnapped the beautiful Helen, wife of the powerful Greek king, Menelaus. Homer's epic poem features brutally realistic battle scenes between heroic characters. These include Agamemnon, the proud leader of the Greek forces and Menelaus's brother, and the brave but doomed King Hector of Troy. Most famous of all was Achilles, the invincible Greek warrior whose only weak spot was his heel. Both dramatic and tragic, *The Iliad* deals with human themes such as pride, courage, honor, and vanity.

The Odyssey is a wonderful adventure story that describes the Greek soldier Odysseus's journey home after the Trojan War. This journey by land and sea takes him ten years. To be reunited with his wife and son, the hero relies on his intelligence and sly trickery to overcome monsters, storms, the anger of the gods, and many other obstacles. Aside from inventing one of the world's most memorable heroes, Homer's tale led to "odyssey" becoming an English word, which is used to describe a great adventurous journey or quest.

for Macedonia is too little for thee." Philip's words would prove to be prophetic. Meanwhile, Alexander named his new horse Bucephalus. From then on, Bucephalus became the young prince's closest companion.

Alexander is seen riding his beloved Bucephalus in this fourteenth-century Greek manuscript by Pseudo-Callisthenes.

When Alexander turned sixteen, Philip believed it was time for his son to learn about warfare. In order to gain military experience, Alexander joined his father's army. At the age of seventeen, the young prince led a successful attack on the armies of Athens and another city-state called Thebes. He was well on his way to proving himself as an intelligent and fearless warrior and military commander.

Four years later, in 336 BCE, Philip was murdered, and Alexander became Macedonia's new king as well as commander in chief of its impressive army. His military experience had left Alexander eager to continue his father's goal of conquering other lands. However, his ambitions were such that he vowed to continue fighting until he had conquered the entire known world.

Waging battle after battle, he led his troops east through Asia. Accompanying him was his constant companion, Bucephalus, and a copy of *The Iliad*, which he placed under his pillow every night. In fact, *The Iliad* was never far from the great warrior's thoughts. Early in his campaign, Alexander had insisted upon visiting the legendary city of Troy. With a few close friends, he sought out the grave of the Greek hero Achilles. According to legend, Alexander uncovered old pieces of armor from the Trojan War. Hoping they would bring him luck, he wore them in battle.

Aristotle's nephew, Callisthenes, was asked to travel with the troops and keep a journal of Alexander's adventures. He was only one of many nonsoldiers that accompanied Alexander and his troops. Others included poets who were hired to compose glorious battle epics, entertain tired soldiers with songs, and recite poetry. Engineers, philosophers, geographers, and natural

At the Battle of Issus in 330 BCE, Alexander the Great defeated Darius III of Persia and continued his conquest into Asia.

scientists also came along to study the different cultures, technologies, traditions, and plant and animal life of the countries conquered.

During his campaign, Alexander never forgot his former tutor. He ordered that Aristotle's hometown of Stagira, which had been severely damaged in a fire, be rebuilt. When he conquered Lesbos, where Aristotle's friend Theophrastus lived, he prohibited his soldiers from looting homes and businesses. He also made sure that the botanists and biologists that accompanied him sent interesting plant and animal specimens back to Aristotle.

Alexander's military campaigns took him all the way to India. Along the way, he conquered many great cities, including Herat (in present-day Afghanistan) and Samarkand (in present-day Uzbekistan). He also founded several new ones. One of the most important was Alexandria, in Egypt, which he named after himself. Strategically situated at the point where the Nile River runs into the Mediterranean Sea, Alexandria soon developed into one of the ancient world's major cultural, intellectual, and commercial centers.

A NEW SCHOOL

Aristotle had not accompanied Alexander on his conquests. After spending some time in Pella and then in Stagira, Aristotle decided to go back to Athens in 335 BCE. His return marked the first time he had been to the city in twelve years. At age fifty, he dreamed of starting his own school— one similar to the Academy—where he could share his knowledge with young students.

At this time, Athens, which was under Macedonian rule, was governed by Alexander. Since Aristotle was not a citizen of Athens, he couldn't buy land for his school. However, with the aid of Macedonian officials, he was able to rent some land outside the city walls. A temple built to honor the god Apollo Lyceus was on the land. Because of this, Aristotle's school came to be called the Lyceum.

CHAPTER FOUR

New Ideas in Science, Logic, and Politics

Aristotle did not set up his new school to be an exact replica of Plato's Academy. While Plato had encouraged discussions and dialogues between students and teachers, Aristotle preferred to focus on lectures and scientific research. According to historical accounts, Aristotle himself was a brilliant and articulate teacher. He often gave his lectures while strolling up and down the path that led to the temple of Apollo Lyceus. His students were forced to follow closely behind if they wanted to hear his lessons in their entirety. They were subsequently called the Peripatetics—Greek for "walkabouts" or "wanderers." The Lyceum itself became known as the Peripatetic School.

THE LYCEUM

Aristotle usually taught more advanced students in the morning. Afternoons were reserved for lectures for the general public. Ultimately, Aristotle spent thirteen years at the Lyceum. It was during this time that he produced most of his written works. Many of his lecture notes were collected and later published. Aristotle also wrote dialogues based on debates he had with his students. Inspired by Plato's dialogues, these works were written in a more common, everyday language than his other works, which tended to be more dense and technical.

Aristotle had always been a great collector of books. When he founded the Lyceum, he created the first great library in Greece. His private collection was enriched by the numerous books that Alexander sent to him from his travels. In fact, Aristotle's library at the Lyceum was the inspiration for the famed library of Alexandria. Aristotle was also able to create an important museum of natural history with the many animal and plant specimens that Alexander sent from faraway lands.

Such resources helped Aristotle attract an impressive array of scholars to the Lyceum. Here, they taught and conducted research. Among them was his old friend from Lesbos, Theophrastus. At the Lyceum, students could learn about every subject imaginable at the time. In the first century BCE, the famous Roman orator Cicero (106 BCE–43 BCE) compared the Lyceum to a factory that produced professionals of every kind: diplomats, military commanders, doctors, engineers, poets, and even

Archaeologists have identified these ruins as part of the Lyceum. The culture ministry of Greece has now opened the site to the public.

musicians. Aristotle himself was often referred to as a polymath, meaning that he had in-depth knowledge on a vast array of subjects.

One of Aristotle's most important contributions at the Lyceum was the development of an early version of the scientific method. In the scientific method, scientists investigate questions by observing and measuring evidence. Only after they have sufficiently tested their hypotheses through experimentation do they come to any kind of conclusion. Although he did not conduct experiments, Aristotle was one of the first philosophers to trust observation over preconceived notions of a particular phenomenon. This method of inquiry not only influenced all teaching and research of the Lyceum, but it also revolutionized Western thinking forever.

HOW TO DRAW LOGICAL CONCLUSIONS

Aristotle claimed that when studying any problem, the first step was to research all available information. It was not enough to simply read this information; one had to examine it

Aristotle is shown working with several students in this thirteenth-century Turkish illustration.

with a critical eye to judge if it made sense. Any doubtful information or faulty conclusions needed to be questioned and reexamined. After coming up with one's own solution to the problem, a good researcher needed to seek evidence that would support his or her point of view, which in turn could (and should) be questioned by other scholars. By following such a rational system of investigation, human knowledge of the world could constantly progress, while flawed conclusions and beliefs could be discarded.

This scientific reasoning—drawing conclusions from factual evidence—is known as logic. Aristotle was the first philosopher to create a formal system of logic that could be used to understand the world. Today, logical thinking has become second nature. For example, if we look out on the window on a winter day and see people walking around wearing hats and scarves, we logically conclude that it is very cold outside. Of course, this is just an assumption based on a piece of evidence. To prove that it really is cold outdoors, we would have to step outside ourselves (preferably with a thermometer) to test the air temperature.

Using logical connections, such as in the previous example, to arrive at a conclusion is known as syllogism. Aristotle's most famous example of syllogism said:

1) All men are mortal (they are born, live, and die).

2) Socrates is a man.

3) Thus, the logical conclusion, based on deduction, is that Socrates is mortal.

The Quotable Aristotle

Although many of Aristotle's texts that survived were unpolished lecture notes, he was known to have been an accomplished teacher with a flair for rhetoric. To this day, many of his wise observations and reflections are frequently quoted. Here are some of the best known:

On humans:

"We are what we repeatedly do."
"All men by nature desire knowledge."

On nature:

"In all things of nature there is something of the marvelous."
"Nature does nothing uselessly."

On education:

"Education is the best provision for old age."
"It is the mark of an educated mind to be able to entertain a thought without accepting it."

On honesty:

"Liars when they speak the truth are not believed."

On poverty:

"Poverty is the parent of revolution and crime."

(continued on the next page)

The Quotable Aristotle (Continued)

On war:

"We make war that we may live in peace."

On law:

"Law is order, and good law is good order."

On democracy:

"The only stable state is the one in which all men are equal before the law."
"The basis of a democratic state is liberty."
"If liberty and equality, as is thought by some, are chiefly to be found in democracy, they will be best attained when all persons alike share in the government to the utmost."

On work:

"Pleasure in the job puts perfection in the work."

On friendship:

"Without friends no one would choose to live, though he had all other goods."
"Misfortune shows those who are not really friends."
"What is a friend? A single soul dwelling in two bodies."

By using logic, Aristotle also believed it was possible to organize the chaos of the world into ordered categories. For instance, he divided all matter on Earth into three groups: animal, vegetable, and mineral. Each main group could be broken down into subcategories based on similarities and differences. An example of this was Aristotle's classification of animals into "bloodless" and "blooded," which were then further divided into other subcategories.

PHYSICS AND *METAPHYSICS*

At the Lyceum, while Aristotle continued to pursue his passion for classifying and studying animals, his friend Theophrastus turned his attention to the vegetable (plants) and mineral groups. In his book *Account of Plants*, Theophrastus succeeded in identifying and describing more than 550 plant species. He divided these into categories such as trees, shrubs, and herbs. This undertaking led Theophrastus to be considered the world's first botanist, or scientist who studies plant life.

Although his great passion was natural science, Aristotle brought new approaches to many other scientific fields. For example, he was the first to distinguish between mathematics and physics as two separate disciplines. Previously, ancient Greek scholars had used mathematics to explain natural occurrences ranging from the arrangement of the stars and planets in the sky to the notes created by musical instruments. Many had been inspired by the teachings of the great sixth century BCE

This is a page from the beginning of Physics, *Aristotle's examination of the causes and changes in the natural world.*

mathematician Pythagoras, who believed that the world could be reduced to numbers and formulas.

However, for Aristotle, mathematics was an abstract science that dealt with shapes, volumes, and calculations. In contrast, physics was a concrete science that explained how and why things functioned as they did and the reasons they changed. Aristotle wrote a series of essays on these questions that were grouped together and published under the title *Physics* (circa 350 BCE).

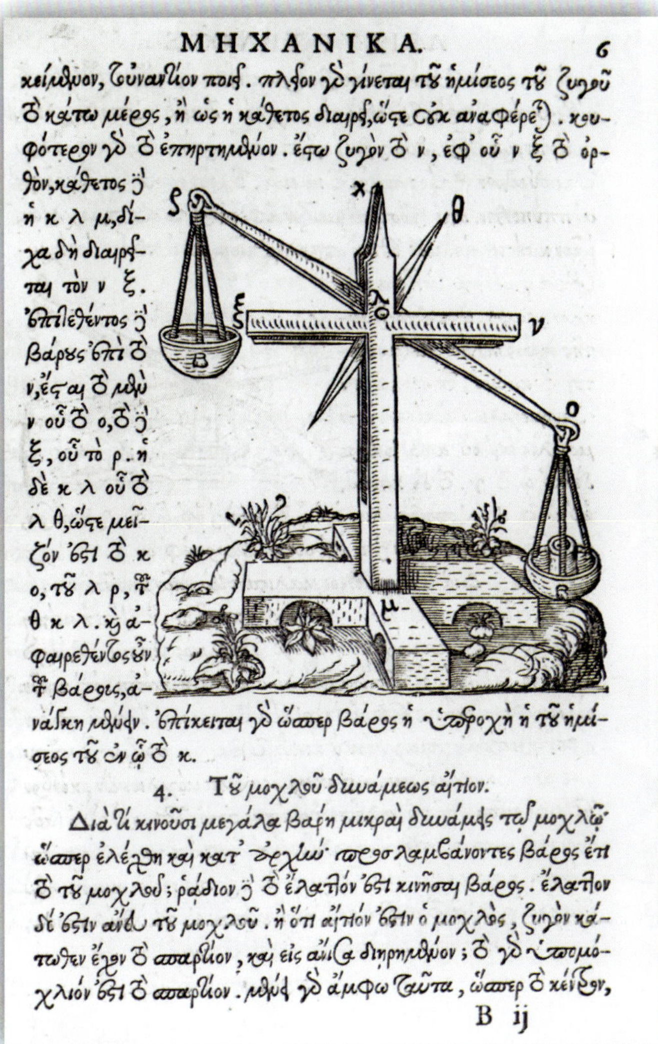
ΜΗΧΑΝΙΚΑ. 6

4. Τοῦ μοχλοῦ δυνάμεως αἴτιον.

B ij

This reproduction of one of Aristotle's manuscripts was published in Paris in 1566.

Aristotle believed that all matter was capable of undergoing four kinds of changes:

TYPE OF CHANGE	EXAMPLE
1) CHANGE IN LOCATION (MOVEMENT)	A ROCK PUSHED FROM A CLIFF INTO A LAKE
2) CHANGE IN QUALITY (ALTERATION)	WATER THAT FREEZES AND BECOMES ICE
3) CHANGE IN SIZE (EXPANSION OR CONTRACTION)	A PIECE OF CHEWING GUM THAT IS STRETCHED INTO A LONG RIBBON
4) CHANGE IN SUBSTANCE	MELTING COPPER AND ZINC TOGETHER TO MAKE BRASS

The first three changes were physical changes. However, when matter changed its very substance, this was a chemical change. For instance, to make bronze, ancient Greeks melted together tin and copper. Once the mixture had solidified, it would no longer be possible to extract either of the original substances (tin or copper) from the new substance (bronze).

According to Aristotle, two elements were involved in any change: the substances that underwent the change and the forces responsible for causing the change. The forces were external. When applied to tin and copper, heat was the force that caused both metals to melt and mix together, becoming bronze. The changing of the seasons and the resulting differences in weather conditions (varying amounts of heat, cold, rain, sunshine, etc.) caused the birth, growth, and death of all plant life.

Molten bronze, created from the combination of tin and copper, is still used to sculpt fine art pieces.

In his book *Meteorology* (circa 350 BCE), Aristotle attempted to explain the changes and forces that affected the Earth. Modern-day meteorology refers to the study of weather, but for Aristotle, it embraced all natural occurrences on the earth ranging from thunder, lightning, winds, and earthquakes (which he thought were caused by underground winds) to ocean tides and tidal waves. Among his important discoveries was that the sun played a key role in the earth's hydraulic (water) cycle. In *Meteorology*, Aristotle explained evaporation and precipitation, stating, "By its [the sun's] agency the finest and sweetest water is every day carried up and is dissolved into vapor and rises to the upper regions, where it is condensed again by the cold and so returns to the earth."

Aristotle encountered difficulty when it came to understanding astronomical phenomena such as stars, comets, and meteors. Since he could find no cause for the movement of these bodies, he had to assume that an "Unmoved Mover," or God, was responsible for these changes. The "Unmoved Mover" was an eternal force. Aristotle wrote about the idea of God in a group of essays called the *Metaphysics* (circa 350 BCE). *Meta* is the Greek work for "after." Fittingly, *Metaphysics* was the book that came after Aristotle's collection of essays entitled *Physics*.

Metaphysics' opening line would become one of Aristotle's most memorable declarations: "All men by nature have a desire for knowledge." Aristotle believed that it was our need to understand things and our ability to think rationally that set human beings apart from the rest of the animal kingdom and brought us closer to God.

CODE OF CONDUCT

Aside from science, Aristotle was interested in many other aspects of human existence. His series of essays on ethics (rules that state how to behave) outlined basic human codes of social conduct. Of his three books on ethics, the most famous is *Nicomachean Ethics* (circa 350 BCE), which Aristotle wrote as a rulebook for his young son, Nicomachus. Following ancient Greek tradition, Aristotle's son had been named in honor of Aristotle's father. He was born to Aristotle's second wife, Herpyllis, a woman from Stagira whom the philosopher had married following the death of his first wife, Pythias.

Aristotle declared that young people, whom he believed to be naturally undisciplined and filled with energy, required strict laws to teach them right from wrong. This kind of knowledge would help them become responsible citizens. Aristotle also believed that the highest goal in a person's life was the pursuit of happiness. People who sought riches and fame and believed that these things would make them happy were mistaken. Happiness, however, was not to be confused with pleasure. Instead, in *Nicomachean Ethics*, Aristotle defined happiness as "an activity of the soul according to goodness in a mature person."

Aristotle also placed a very high value on friendship. "Without friends no one would choose to live, though he had all other goods," he wrote in *Nicomachean Ethics*. Known for his lifelong friendships with many men, such as Theosphratus, Aristotle practiced what he preached.

AN IDEAL GOVERNMENT

Aristotle lived during turbulent political times. As a friend and tutor of Alexander, he had firsthand experience of the workings of governments led by kings and tyrants. Living in democratic Athens allowed Aristotle to observe the world's first citizens' government ruled by popular assembly. At the same time, he witnessed the constant threats to democracy. Aristotle analyzed the impacts these different forms of government had on human lives. Based on his observations, he constructed his ideas of an ideal society governed by an ideal form of government.

Since he thrived as a teacher and intellectual under Athenian democracy, it was no surprise that Aristotle championed a democratic state in which all men were free and equal and allowed to participate in their own government. He also believed that a state, or nation, was not merely a community of people that banded together for defensive and commercial reasons, but rather a society whose goal should be "noble actions." By this, he meant that individuals had a duty to work together in order to create a better, more harmonious society.

THEATER IN THE COMMUNITY

Theater played an enormous role in Greek life. In ancient Athens, theaters themselves were important public monuments, and playwrights were highly respected members of society. Great playwrights such as Sophocles (circa 496 BCE–406 BCE) and Euripides (circa 480 BCE–406 BCE) often inserted philosophical arguments into the text of their comedies and tragedies. Aside from becoming emotionally engaged, the public was meant to reflect upon the serious issues addressed in a play.

In *Poetics*, Aristotle developed very precise theories about theater, specifically tragedy. He felt that a proper tragedy was made up of six key elements: plot, character, diction (speech), thought, spectacle, and song. The plot should be about one important subject. Unlike comedies, which were meant to have happy endings, a tragedy traced the downfall of the main character. The downfall was usually brought about by a serious flaw or weakness (such as stubbornness or excessive pride) in the heroic character.

Since Aristotle thought the most important human goal was the pursuit of happiness, how could he justify the value of a tragedy that made people feel sad or despairing? He reasoned that in watching the downfall of a noble character, audience members were able to relieve themselves of feelings of fear and pity. In other words, after viewing a tragic play, audience members felt a positive sensation of relief. Aristotle called this sensation a "catharsis."

Originally, catharsis was a medical term that referred to purging dangerous elements in a person's body that were causing illness. Aristotle believed that if everyone in the audience watching a play experienced a catharsis, this would result in a common bond that would reinforce a sense of community.

In *Poetics*, Aristotle also discussed two other important types of writing: poetry and history. He claimed that the difference between the two was more

Many ancient Greek theaters still survive, such as this one in Epidaurus.

than the obvious fact that one was written in verse and the other in prose. Aristotle pointed out that while history deals with facts from the past, poetry concerns itself with imagining the possibilities of the future. He concluded that poetry was a superior art since it deals with universal human issues, while history simply relates details of events that have already taken place.

that they had already reached the end of the world. Hence, after setting the Indian king free and founding a city—named Bucephala (present-day Jhelum in Pakistan) in honor of his faithful horse—Alexander began leading his exhausted troops back to Greece. Weakened and weary, he never completed the long trip home. After coming down with a severe fever (probably malaria), he died in Babylon in 323 BCE.

Because Alexander didn't have any children or heirs, there was no one to take his place as ruler of an enormous empire. Without a strong central power, wars broke out between the leaders of various territories. The empire soon began to fall apart. Nonetheless, Alexander's conquests had permanently changed the world. The thousands of Macedonians and Greeks who had traveled with him on his campaign settled in the new cities he had founded in places as far-flung as Egypt, Syria, and Persia. As a result, Greek culture took root and had a long-lasting impact in these lands.

ARISTOTLE'S LAST YEARS

When news of the death of Alexander reached Athens, most Athenians were happy. They had resented the Macedonian conquest of their formerly independent city. With hostilities on the rise, many Macedonians decided to leave the city. Aristotle was very well respected in Athens. However, his relationship with Alexander, as well as the generous contributions Alexander had made to the Lyceum, was public knowledge. As a result,

Though Aristotle was long revered as the greatest philosopher of all time, many scientists by the seventeenth century, when this engraving was made, viewed his work with skepticism.

some important Athenians doubted his loyalty. Because Aristotle was so famous, he became an easy target for anti-Macedonian sentiment.

It wasn't long before the same charges that had been brought against Socrates were being leveled at Aristotle. Remembering the fate of Socrates, Aristotle vowed that he wouldn't give the Athenians another chance to, as he put it, "sin against philosophy." Instead of waiting for his trial, he fled Athens with his wife and two children and escaped to Euboea. In the town of Chalcis, he and his family settled in the house that had once belonged to his mother. Less than a year after going into exile, Aristotle became ill with stomach pains and a fever. He died in 322 BCE at the age of sixty-two.

When Aristotle departed from Athens, he had left the Lyceum in the care of Theophrastus. As well, he left him in charge of his personal library, which included all his lecture notes, books, and research.

PRESERVING ARISTOTLE'S WORK

When Theophrastus died in 287 BCE, he left Aristotle's library to his nephew, Neleus, who lived in the town of Scepsis, in Asia Minor. After Neleus's death, what happened to Aristotle's writings is somewhat of a mystery. According to some historians, Neleus's relatives sold many of his manuscripts to the great library at Alexandria. They hid other texts in a cave. Two centuries later, a book collector named Apellico was traveling through Scepsis and heard tales about these buried manuscripts. After

Aristotle's Biographer

A Greek historian named Diogenes Laertius, who lived in the third century CE (five hundred years after Aristotle), was the first to write a biography about the major Greek philosophers. Diogenes describes Aristotle as a somewhat elegant man who stood out in a crowd due to his clothing and jewelry and the way he cut his hair. He apparently had very thin legs and spoke with a lisp. According to Diogenes, Aristotle was a kind man who was generous to his family and friends. Although he had a serious nature, he had a good sense of humor and was known to joke with his colleagues and students.

uncovering them, he took them back to his own private library in Athens.

In 84 BCE, a Roman general named Sulla led an invasion of Athens. Once the city was under Roman control, Sulla seized Apellico's precious collection and took them to a library in Rome. They were forgotten for years until they came to the attention of Cicero, a famous Roman writer and politician. He recognized they were the works of a great philosopher. Cicero praised Aristotle's ideas and quoted him extensively in his own writings, which were widely read and respected in Rome.

Marcus Tullius Cicero (106 BCE–43 BCE) was a Roman politician whose work on philosophy was highly influenced by Aristotle's writings.

As such, Aristotle's teachings were diffused throughout the Roman Empire.

Shortly after, around 30 BCE, a scholar named Andronicus from the Greek island of Rhodes decided to edit all of Aristotle's surviving works. All in all, according to Aristotle's first biographer, Diogenes Laertius (circa 200–300 CE), the philosopher had written over 150 titles. Most of these, however, had been handwritten on scrolls made of fragile parchment paper. Unfortunately, many were lost or damaged over time. In fact, none of the books Aristotle wrote while he was at the Academy survived. Luckily, these manuscripts were read by other scholars, who copied down or quoted portions of the originals in their own works. The majority of Aristotle's surviving texts consisted of the lecture notes he wrote during his years in Assos, in Pella, and at the Lyceum.

For a long time, Aristotle's theories were much less influential than those of his master, Plato. After the fall of the Roman Empire in 476 CE, his works were scarcely read in Europe. However, in the Middle East, Arab scholars highly valued his teachings. When Arabs invaded Europe in the twelfth and thirteenth centuries, Aristotle was rediscovered in Europe. His works were translated into Latin, the major written language in Europe at the time, and his theories became incredibly influential. While many of Plato's teachings lost favor with European scholars, Aristotle came to be considered the greatest philosopher of all time.

THE IMPORTANCE OF QUESTIONING

During the Middle Ages, the title of "the Philosopher" was given to Aristotle by Scholastic thinkers who mixed his philosophy with Christian beliefs. His theories were embraced by the Catholic Church, which had become increasingly popular. As a result, Aristotle's views were considered to be sacred, so much so that his writings carried the same authority as the Bible. Even observations of his that were quite incorrect could not be questioned by other scholars or philosophers. To criticize Aristotle's beliefs was considered a sin. This was ironic since Aristotle firmly believed in the importance of challenging authority. For him, questioning established facts was an essential means of discovering new knowledge.

Today, many scholars believe that this absolute belief in Aristotle's theories hindered scientific progress in the West for centuries. In fact, until the scientific revolution of the sixteenth and seventeenth centuries, scientists risked their lives whenever they publicly proposed theories that conflicted with Aristotle's.

GALILEO'S EXPERIMENTATION

The great Italian astronomer and physicist Galileo Galilei (1564–1642) was among the first to challenge Aristotelian ideas. One of the pioneers of modern science, Galileo used the scientific method of experimentation to solve problems. Unlike Aristotle, Galileo believed one couldn't reach a conclusion simply by using reason and logic. It

The front cover of Systema Cosmicum, *Galileo's 1663 treatise, depicts Aristotle, Ptolemy, and Nicolaus Copernicus, other thinkers who had studied the solar system.*

was necessary to prove a conclusion by means of actual experimentation. Aristotle claimed that observing a thing made it real. Galileo countered that a thing could only be considered real if it had been measured and quantified.

Galileo did just this when he dropped two different-sized cannonballs from the Leaning Tower of Pisa and discovered that objects of different masses fall at the same speed. Aristotle had said quite the contrary. Based on logic, he believed that if one dropped two balls, and one was twice as heavy as the other, the heavier ball would fall twice as fast as the lighter ball. However, Aristotle had never backed up his theory by providing actual evidence. Had he performed such an experiment, he would have easily seen that his theory was wrong. Both balls would have hit the ground at almost the same time.

Galileo got into trouble for challenging another of Aristotle's "truths"—that of a geocentric universe (*geo* is Greek for "Earth"). According to this theory, Earth was the center of the world around which all other planets revolved. Galileo echoed the views of Polish astronomer Nicolaus Copernicus (1473–1543), who had proposed a heliocentric universe with planets, including Earth, revolving around the sun (*helio* is the Greek word for "sun"). Both men reached their conclusions with the aid of the newly invented telescope. Nonetheless, their theories were viewed as criminal in the eyes of the Catholic Church. The church firmly believed in Aristotle's statement that Earth is the center of the universe. After bringing Galileo to trial, the church

Assessing Aristotle's Natural Science

By the nineteenth century, scientific advancements had disproved many of Aristotle's theories. In one field, though, he was recognized as an important pioneer. Biologists and zoologists in the late nineteenth century rediscovered and applauded Aristotle's observations concerning the natural sciences. A great admirer of Aristotle's was the famous naturalist Charles Darwin, whose landmark book *On the Origin of Species* (1859) elaborated the theory of the evolution of species.

Darwin was impressed by Aristotle's thorough classification and descriptions of animals. He was also amazed at how much common knowledge had been based on Aristotle's theories. Indeed, some of Aristotle's more abstract ideas contained in *Ethics, Politics, and Poetics* (in which he examines timeless human issues such as pleasure, honor, art, justice, and democracy) are still very influential today.

On the other hand, it is undeniable that some of Aristotle's theories about animals were very flawed, as scientists eventually discovered. Without the aid of sophisticated scientific equipment such as microscopes, Aristotle sometimes arrived at incorrect conclusions.

(*continued on the next page*)

ASSESSING ARISTOTLE'S NATURAL SCIENCE (CONTINUED)

For example, because he couldn't see their tiny eggs, he thought that some insects had no parents and emerged as full-grown adults from decomposing plants and the bodies of other animals. He was confused about whether dolphins breathed water or air, and he believed that honeybees flying in strong winds carried stones in order to balance their flight. Overall, however, his knowledge of the animal world was remarkably accurate given his limited ability to observe it.

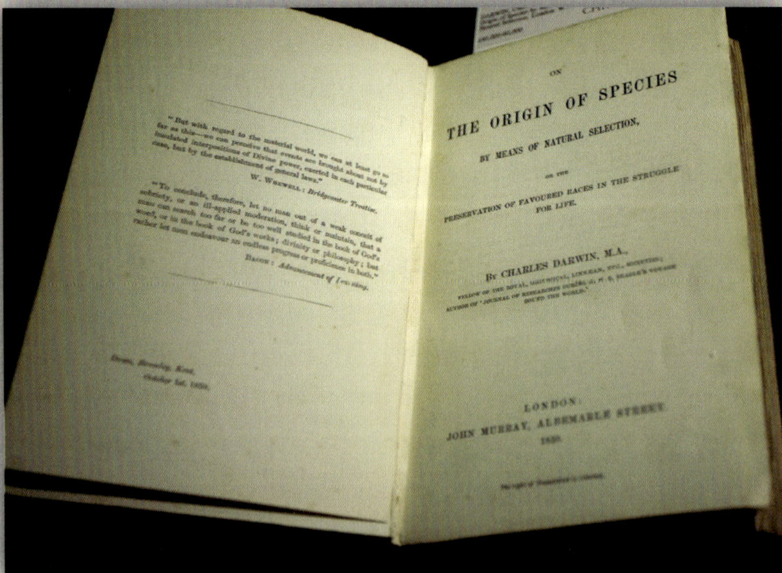

This rare first edition of Darwin's On the Origin of Species *sold for over $170,000 at an auction in 2009.*

forced him to reject his own beliefs of a sun-centered universe and then sentenced him to life imprisonment.

The belief in such inaccurate theories led many scholars in the seventeenth and eighteenth centuries to regard Aristotle as a deeply flawed scientist. Many scientists rejected Aristotle's beliefs in favor of exploring new theories and methods.

ARISTOTLE LIVES ON

Scientists now recognize that Aristotle was wrong about many things. Yet, by developing a system of logical thinking, Aristotle himself laid the groundwork for future thinkers to disprove his work. In fact, philosophers often define contemporary Western thought as "Aristotelian" because it has become second nature for people to think of the world around them in terms of facts and scientific categories.

When people don't understand something, they automatically search for reasonable and logical explanations based on physical evidence. They make lists and collect information. They try to classify things to give order and meaning to their lives. They rely on their senses—hearing, touch, smell, taste, and sight—to make sense of the external world. When they have a problem, they try to reason out a way to a solution. All of these methods are so natural to people that this type of thinking is referred to as common sense. Ultimately, in some ways, common sense wouldn't exist if it hadn't been for Aristotle.

The system of logical reasoning that Aristotle pioneered later evolved into the modern scientific method:

Timeline

384 BCE Aristotle is born in Stagira, a Greek colony in northern Greece, near the kingdom of Macedonia.

374 BCE Aristotle's father, Nicomachus, dies. A close family friend, Proxenus, becomes his guardian.

367 BCE At age seventeen, Aristotle is sent to Athens to study at Plato's Academy.

347 BCE Plato dies. Aristotle leaves Athens. He travels to Asia Minor (now Turkey) and settles at the court of Hermias. He marries Hermias's niece, Pythias. Shortly after she gives birth to a daughter, also named Pythias.

344 BCE After Hermias is murdered, Aristotle and his family move to Lesbos, where he begins his studies of land and sea creatures.

343 BCE Aristotle is invited to Macedonia to tutor Alexander, teenage son of Philip II, king of Macedonia.

338 BCE Philip takes control of all of Greece, including Athens.

336 BCE After Philip II is murdered, Alexander becomes king of Macedonia and sets off to conquer the known world.

335 BCE Aristotle returns to Athens and creates his own school, the Lyceum. Here he lectures, founds a museum and a library, and writes many of his famous works.

323 BCE Alexander the Great dies, and the fall of his empire begins. There are revolts against Macedonians in Athens. Charged with "impiety," Aristotle flees Athens and settles in Chalcis on the island of Euboea.

322 BCE Aristotle dies on Euboea at the age of sixty-two, after complaining of a stomach illness. He leaves behind his second wife, Herpyllis; Nicomachus, the son they had together; and his daughter, Pythias.

Glossary

ARTICULATE Able to express oneself powerfully, using clear, precise language.

ASSEMBLY A public gathering of citizens to discuss and vote upon laws for governing a city or state.

ASSUMPTION Something taken for granted or accepted as true without proof.

AUTHORITARIAN Relating to absolute and strict obedience.

CATHARSIS A positive sense of relief, or the removal of dangerous elements in the body that are causing illness.

CITY-STATE A city that exists as an individual state or country.

DEDUCTION An inference based on logic or established principles.

DICTION A careful, correct speaking style with an emphasis on choice of words.

EPIC Something heroic and impressive that celebrates a legendary moment or event; can refer specifically to a long narrative poem written in a grand style with a heroic theme.

ETHICS A set of rules of good conduct; a system of moral values.

HEMLOCK Deadly liquid poison derived from the hemlock plant.

MALARIA An infectious and often deadly disease spread by mosquitoes in tropical climates.

MATTER A physical substance that occupies space and can be perceived by the senses.

OBJECTIVE Having to do with a real, material object that can be perceived.

ORATOR A skilled public speaker.

POLYMATH A person who has great knowledge on a variety of different topics.

PROPHETIC Predicting events to come.

RATIONAL Based on reason or logic.

REPROVE To criticize, scold, or disapprove of.

RHETORIC In ancient Greece, the art of persuasive public speaking; in modern times, it refers to both oral and written communication.

ROUSE To stir to action.

SCHOLASTIC THINKERS The dominant school of philosophers in Europe during the Middle Ages, who adhered to Aristotle's theories and Christian beliefs.

SUBJECTIVE Having to do with an idea imagined by an individual; something that comes from a person's mind instead of from the real, material world.

SYLLOGISM A form of reasoning that uses logical connections between two or more assumed statements in order to come to a conclusion.

TYRANT An absolute ruler who governs without limits.

UPHEAVAL A violent disruption or upsetting event.

For More Information

The American Classical League (ACL)

Miami University

422 Wells Mill Drive

Oxford, OH 45056

(513) 529-7741

Website: http://www.aclclassics.org

The ACL is dedicated to promoting the study of classical Greek and Latin language and culture at all academic levels. In addition to sponsoring national exams, the ACL offers several scholarships to students and teachers of classics as well as placement assistance for educators

American Philosophical Society

104 South Fifth Street

Philadelphia, PA 19106-3387

(215) 440-3400

Website: http://www.amphilsoc.org

Founded in 1743, the American Philosophical Society is the oldest learned society in the United States. It promotes knowledge in the sciences and humanities through research, meetings, publications, and community outreach.

The Aristotelian Society
Room 260, Senate House
Malet Street
London WC1E 7HU
England
Website: https://www.aristoteliansociety.org.uk

The Aristotelian Society was founded in 1880 by five men, including a chemist, a Shakespeare scholar, and a socialist activist, who were interested in studying all aspects of philosophy, just as Aristotle did. Today it hosts philosophical talks every two weeks during the academic year, which are free, open to the public, and later published.

The Center for Hellenic Studies
3100 Whitehaven Street NW
Washington, DC 20008
(202) 745-4400
Website: http://www.chs.harvard.edu

The Center for Hellenic Studies deals with research and teaching in all aspects of Hellenic civilization, including Greek language and interaction with foreign culture. It has also expanded into online classes, books, and publications.

The Classical Association of Canada
Université Laval
Département d'histoire 1030
av. des Sciences-Humaines
Québec, QC G1V 0A6
Canada
Website: http://cac-scec.ca/wordpress/index
The Classical Association of Canada advances the study of the Greek and Roman civilizations and their later influence on modern culture, encouraging the teaching of classical languages and civilizations in Canadian education at all levels.

The Metropolitan Museum of Art
Greek and Roman Art Department
1000 Fifth Avenue at 82nd Street
New York, NY 10028
(212) 535-7710

Website: http://www.metmuseum.org

The Metropolitan Museum of Art has the largest collection of Greek and Roman art in North America with over seventeen thousand items. Dating from 4500 BCE to 312 CE, its works cover a wide geographical area that includes Cyprus and Asia Minor in addition to modern-day Greece and Italy.

The Society for Classical Studies

University of Pennsylvania

220 S. 40th Street, Suite 201E

Philadelphia, PA 19104-3512

(215) 898-4975

Website: http://www.apaclassics.org

Originally founded in 1869 as the American Philological Association, the Society for Classical Studies promotes the study of ancient Greek and Roman languages, literatures, and civilizations. It produces scholarly journals, fosters wider public appreciation of the classics, and coordinates activities for teaching the classics to students of all ages.

The Stavros Niarchos Foundation Centre for Hellenic Studies
Simon Fraser University
8888 University Drive
Burnaby, BC V5A 1S6
Canada
Website: http://www.sfu.ca/snfchs.html

This center supports the teaching of Greek history, language, and culture through teaching and research. Via its New Media Lab, the center offers online tutoring in Greek, a guide to the city of Athens, and other e-learning projects.

WEBSITES

Because of the changing nature of Internet links, Rosen Publishing has developed an online list of websites related to the subject of this book. This site is updated regularly. Please use this link to access the list:

http://www.rosenlinks.com/GGP/Aris

For Further Reading

Anderson, Margaret J., and Karen F. Stephenson. *Aristotle: Genius Philosopher and Scientist* (Genius Scientists and Their Genius Ideas). Berkeley Heights, NJ: Enslow Publishers, 2015.

Aristotle. *The Complete Works of Aristotle: The Revised Oxford Translation*. Jonathan Barnes, ed. Princeton, NJ: Princeton University Press, 2014.

Bruell, Christopher. *Aristotle as Teacher: His Introduction to a Philosophic Science*. South Bend, IN: St. Augustine's Press, 2014.

DK Publishing. *Heads Up Philosophy*. New York, NY: DK Publishing, 2014.

DK Publishing. *The Philosophy Book* (Big Ideas Simply Explained). New York, NY: DK Publishing, 2011

Duignan, Brian, ed. *Ancient Philosophy: From 600 BCE to 500 CE* (The History of Philosophy). New York, NY: Britannica Educational Publishing, 2010.

Freeman, Philip. *Alexander the Great*. New York, NY: Simon & Schuster, 2011.

Goldstein, Rebecca Newberger. *Plato at the Googleplex: Why Philosophy Won't Go Away*. New York, NY: Pantheon, 2014.

Herman, Arthur. *The Cave and the Light: Plato Versus Aristotle, and the Struggle for the Soul of Western Civilization*. New York, NY: Random House, 2013.

Johnson, David M. *Socrates and Athens* (Greece & Rome: Texts and Contexts). New York, NY: Cambridge University Press, 2011.

Kenny, Anthony. *A New History of Western Philosophy*. Reprint edition. New York, NY: Oxford University Press, 2012.

Kleinman, Paul. *Philosophy 101*. Avon, MA: Adams Media, 2013.

Kuiper, Kathleen. *Ancient Greece: From the Archaic Period to the Death of Alexander the Great*. New York, NY: Britannica Educational Publishing, 2015.

Leroi, Armand Marie. *The Lagoon: How Aristotle Invented Science*. New York, NY: Viking, 2014.

Martin, Thomas R., and Christopher W. Blackwell. *Alexander the Great: The Story of an Ancient Life*. New York, NY: Cambridge University Press, 2012.

Morgan, Kathryn. *Discovering Ancient Greece* (Exploring Ancient Civilizations). New York, NY: Britannica Educational Publishing, 2015.

Natali, Carlo. *Aristotle: His Life and School*. D.S.

Hutchinson, ed. Princeton, NJ: Princeton University Press, 2013.

Plato. *Great Dialogues of Plato*. W.H.D. Rouse, trans. New York, NY: Signet Classics, 2015.

Warburton, Nigel. *Philosophy: The Basics*. New York, NY: Routledge, 2012.

Worthington, Ian. *By the Spear: Philip II, Alexander the Great, and the Rise and Fall of Macedonian Civilization* (Ancient Warfare and Civilization). New York, NY: Oxford University Press, 2014.

Bibliography

Anderson, Margaret, and Karen Stephenson. *Aristotle: Philosopher and Scientist*. Berkeley Heights, NJ: Enslow Publishers, 2004.

BBC Schools. "Ancient Greeks: Athens." Retrieved November 17, 2014 (http://www.bbc.co.uk/schools/ancientgreece/athens/index.shtml).

Code, Alan D. *Aristotle*. Boulder, CO: Westview Press, 2003.

Hakim, Joy. *The Story of Science: Aristotle Leads the Way*. Washington, DC: Smithsonian Books, 2004.

History for Kids. "Aristotle." Retrieved November 17, 2014 (http://www.historyforkids.org/learn/greeks/philosophy/aristotle.htm).

Kids' Philosophy Slam. "Aristotle." Retrieved November 17, 2014 (http://www.philosophyslam.org/aristotle.html).

Leroi, Armand Marie. *The Lagoon: How Aristotle Invented Science*. New York, NY: Viking, 2014.

PBS. "The Greeks: Crucible of Civilization." Retrieved November 17, 2014 (http://www.pbs.org/empires/thegreeks/htmlver/).

Sedley, David. *The Cambridge Companion to Greek and Roman Philosophy*. New York, NY: Cambridge University Press, 2003.

Stanford Encyclopedia of Philosophy. "Aristotle's

Ethics." April 21, 2014. Retrieved November 17, 2014 (http://plato.stanford.edu/entries/aristotle-ethics/).

Stanford Encyclopedia of Philosophy. "Aristotle's Logic." March 23, 2011. Retrieved November 17, 2014 (http://plato.stanford.edu/entries/aristotle-logic/).

Stanford Encyclopedia of Philosophy. "Aristotle's Metaphysics." June 11, 2012. Retrieved November 17, 2014 (http://plato.stanford.edu/entries/aristotle-metaphysics/).

Stanford Encyclopedia of Philosophy. "Aristotle's Political Theory." January 26, 2011. Retrieved November 17, 2014 (http://plato.stanford.edu/entries/aristotle-politics/).

Stanford Encyclopedia of Philosophy. "Aristotle's Rhetoric." February 1, 2010. Retrieved November 17, 2014 (http://plato.stanford.edu/entries/aristotle-rhetoric).

Sykka, Iota. "Aristotle's Lyceum in Athens Almost Ready to Open to Public." *International New York Times*, Kathimerini English Edition, June 3, 2014. Retrieved February 19, 2015 (http://www.ekathimerini.com/4Dcgi/4dcgi/_w_articles_wsite4_1_03/06/2014_540206).

University of California, Berkeley Museum of Paleontology. "Aristotle." Retrieved November 17, 2014 (http://www.ucmp.berkeley.edu/history/aristotle.html).

Williams, Brian. *Aristotle*. Chicago, IL: Heinemann Library, 2002.

Woodfin, Rupert. *Introducing Aristotle*. New York, NY: Totem Books, 2001.

Index

ABOUT THE AUTHOR

Like Aristotle was, Kelly Roscoe has long been fascinated by all living creatures, especially ducks and loons. Her interest in philosophy stems from a Western civilization class she took in college. Born in Vermont's Northeast Kingdom, she now lives and writes in Maine.

Mick Isle has written several books for young adults. Since acquiring a degree in journalism from Trinity College in Dublin, Ireland—where he also took many courses in philosophy and ancient Greek civilization—Mick has worked consistently as a journalist, both in his native Ireland and in the United States.

PHOTO CREDITS

Cover Print Collector/Hulton Fine Art Collection/Getty Images; pp. 1, 3, 6–7 (background) Madredus/Shutterstock.com; p. 7 Imagno/Hulton Archive/Getty Images; pp. 10, 21, 38, 57, 76 © dra_schwartz/iStock/Getty Images; p. 11 Chuong Vu/Moment Open/Getty Images; p. 14 Originally published in Historical Atlas of the World, © J. Cappelens Forlag A/S, Oslo, 1962. Maps by Berit Lie. Used with permission of J. W. Cappelens Forlag; pp. 16–17 Scott E Barbour/ Digital Vision/Getty Images; pp. 18, 30–31 Leemage/UIG /Getty Images; p. 23 DEA/G. Dagli Orti/De Agostini/Getty Images; pp. 26–27 Metropolitan Museum of Art, New York USA/ Bridgeman Images; pp. 32–33 Chicago History Museum/Archive Photos/Getty Images; p. 33 Chicago Historical Society/UIG/Getty Images; p. 36 SuperStock; pp. 38–39 Heritage Images/ Hulton Archive/Getty Images; pp. 42–43 Robert Harding/Digital Vision/Getty Images; p. 46 Wild Horizon/UIG/Getty Images; p. 49 Stock Montage/Archive Photos/Getty Images; p. 52 DEA/A. Dagli Orti/De Agostini/Getty Images; pp. 54–55 PHAS/UIG/Getty Images; p. 59 © AP Images; pp. 60–61 Topkapi Palace Museum, Istanbul, Turkey/Bridgeman Images; p. 66 DEA/ J. W. Bulloz /De Agostini/Getty Images; p. 67 De Agostini Picture Library/Getty Images; p. 69 John Burke/Photographer's Choice/Getty Images; pp. 74–75 Education Images/UIG/Getty Images; p. 79 Private Collection/Bridgeman Images; p. 82 Getty Images; p. 85 Science & Society Picture Library/Getty Images; p. 88 John Phillips/UK Press/Getty Images.

Designer: Brian Garvey; Editor: Meredith Day